PROJECT 2025 BREAKDOWN

A Condensed and Simplified Version of the 900-Page Report

Simon C Randy

Disclaimer:

This book contains a condensed and simplified interpretation of topics related to Project 2025. It is intended for informational purposes only. The author and publisher are not affiliated with, endorsed by, or officially associated with Project 2025 or any related entities. While every effort has been made to ensure accuracy, this work should not be considered an official representation or complete account of the original Project 2025 material. Readers are encouraged to consult the original sources for comprehensive details.

FOREWORD

The decision to create a concise version of Project 2025 was driven by the recognition that its vision, goals, and strategies need to be accessible to a broader audience. As the United States faces pivotal challenges ahead of its 250th anniversary, the ideas contained within this project offer vital guidance for navigating the complexities of modern governance. However, the original document is extensive, and many who could benefit from its insights may not have the time or resources to engage with it fully.

This summary distills the core principles and actionable recommendations of Project 2025 into a more manageable format, ensuring that its most important ideas reach those who seek to understand and apply them. By highlighting the key points—such as the need for a streamlined executive branch, the importance of political appointees, and the dangers of unchecked bureaucracy—this summary preserves the essence of the original work while making it more accessible.

Our hope is that this condensed version will serve as a useful tool for policymakers, political leaders, and engaged citizens who are eager to protect America's founding principles. In an era where misinformation and political complexity can obscure the path forward, clear and concise communication is essential. Through this summary, we aim to ensure that Project 2025 continues to inspire, inform, and guide those committed to restoring constitutional governance in the United States.

This foreword serves as a call to action: to take these simplified ideas and translate them into meaningful changes that will shape the future of our nation. By making this project's goals easier to understand and implement, we hope to foster a more informed public and more decisive leadership in the years to come.

As we look to the future, this document provides a vision rooted in the past—a vision that draws upon the values of the Founding Fathers, the wisdom of the Constitution, and the enduring belief in the principles of self-governance. The contributors to this project recognize that America's best days can still be ahead, but only if we commit ourselves to the hard work of preserving the freedoms and liberties that define us.

Table of Contents

INTRODUCTION TO PROJECT 2025

A comprehensive handbook, spanning close to 1,000 pages, has been released by The Heritage Foundation, a conservative think tank, in collaboration with what they describe as a "wide-ranging alliance" of other groups. This document outlines the steps for executing "Project 2025."

According to the creators of Project 2025, this guide is intended to direct the incoming president on reversing what they assert are the negative impacts inflicted on America by liberal politicians. However, detractors argue that Project 2025 represents extremist, "authoritarian" viewpoints and even threatens to be dystopian.

The United States and the conservative movement have been through tough times before, particularly forty-four years ago. Both found themselves in a position of internal fragmentation, external threats, and betrayal by the Washington establishment. The late 1970s were a period of uncertainty and decline for America, marked by economic stagnation, cultural shifts, and growing distrust in the nation's leadership. This era tested the core principles of the conservative movement and the country's ability to preserve its unique legacy of freedom and human flourishing. Yet, as history shows, this difficult time became a turning point that led to significant political, economic, and cultural victories.

During the late 1970s, the United States was confronted with a range of existential threats, both foreign and domestic. The political landscape was marked by stagflation—a troubling combination of stagnant economic growth and high inflation—and gas shortages that left Americans waiting in long lines just to fill their tanks. Internationally, the Soviet Union was on the rise, with the Red Army's invasion of Afghanistan serving as a stark reminder of the global Cold War tensions. Domestically, the country grappled with social and cultural upheaval, as the permissiveness of the 1970s "radical chic" movement began to manifest in various ways throughout American society. The conservative movement itself was splintered and adrift, unsure of how to confront these mounting challenges. Yet, amid this moment of vulnerability and uncertainty, an opportunity for unity and renewal emerged.

As with many historical moments of crisis, the late 1970s became the breeding ground for a conservative renaissance. The Heritage Foundation, a conservative think tank, played a pivotal role in shaping the direction of the movement during this time. In early 1979, as America was gripped by economic turmoil and geopolitical uncertainty, the Heritage Foundation launched a project known as "Mandate for Leadership." This ambitious undertaking brought together hundreds of conservative scholars and academics with the goal of crafting a comprehensive policy agenda that could reform the federal government and rescue the nation from dysfunction.

The result of this collaboration was a 20-volume, 3,000-page handbook filled with more than 2,000 conservative policy recommendations. The Mandate for Leadership represented a promise from the conservative movement to the American people—one that was clear, confident, and specific in its vision for the country's future. This policy blueprint was published in January 1981, just as Ronald Reagan was being sworn in as the 40th president of the United States. By the end of Reagan's first year in office, more than 60 percent of the recommendations outlined in the Mandate for Leadership had been implemented. Under Reagan's leadership, the country began to recover from stagflation, and American confidence and prosperity were revived. Additionally, Reagan's hardline stance in the Cold War contributed to the eventual defeat of the Soviet Union, ending the decades-long geopolitical conflict between the two superpowers.

The success of the Mandate for Leadership and the broader Reagan Revolution is a testament to the power of strategic clarity and bold conservative policy initiatives. However, the challenges facing America today, while different in some ways, echo those of the late 1970s. Once again, the political establishment and cultural elites have driven the country toward decline. Inflation is devastating family budgets, drug overdose deaths are rising, and children are being exposed to increasingly toxic cultural influences, such as the normalization of transgenderism and the introduction of drag queens and pornography into school libraries. Internationally, the Communist dictatorship in Beijing is engaged in a strategic, cultural, and economic Cold War against America's interests, values, and people. Despite this growing threat, the globalist elites in Washington have been slow to respond, and many low-income communities across the country are being devastated by addiction and government dependence.

Adding to these problems is the rise of what has been called "The Great Awokening," a modern-day form of totalitarianism that repurposes the worst elements of 1970s radicalism to create a dangerous and divisive cultural movement. In response to these challenges, the Republican Party seems to lack a clear understanding of what needs to be done. Most alarming of all, the very moral foundations of American society are in peril. Yet, just as the political Right in the late 1970s found a way to unify and lead the country to success, conservatives today must do the same. The lessons of history remind us that, despite the challenges, victory is possible when there is a clear plan, strong leadership, and unity of purpose.

The Heritage Foundation, once again, is stepping up to play a central role in shaping the future of the conservative movement. In April 2022, the Heritage Foundation launched the 2025 Presidential Transition Project, an initiative designed to prepare the next conservative president to take office and implement a bold policy agenda from day one. The first step in this ambitious project is a volume titled "The Conservative Promise," which serves as the opening salvo of the 2025 Presidential Transition Project. This book contains 30 chapters and hundreds of clear, concrete policy recommendations for the White House, Cabinet departments, Congress, and various federal agencies, commissions, and boards.

What sets "The Conservative Promise" apart is not just the scope of its policy recommendations, but also the breadth of its authorship. The book is the product of more than 400 scholars and policy experts from across the conservative movement and the country. Contributors include former elected officials, world-renowned economists, and veterans from four presidential administrations. This collective effort has produced an agenda designed by and for conservatives, ensuring that the next administration will be ready on day one to take decisive action and save the country from its current trajectory of decline.

KEY FIGURES BEHIND PROJECT 2025

Project 2025 was spearheaded by The Heritage Foundation, a prominent conservative think tank. They partnered with a broad coalition of over 70 right-leaning organizations and individuals committed to shaping the future of American governance. Some notable contributors include:

Daren Bakst is currently the Deputy Director for the Center for Energy and Environment at the Competitive Enterprise Institute (CEI). Before joining CEI, he held a significant position at The Heritage Foundation, where he played a key role in the launch of the organization's energy and environmental center. He spent ten years at Heritage, during which time he became a prominent voice in food and agricultural policy, editing and co-authoring Farms and Free Enterprise, a notable publication from the institution. Bakst has testified before Congress multiple times and has taken on leadership roles in several professional organizations, including the Federalist Society and the American Agricultural Law Association.

Jonathan Berry is the managing partner at Boyden Gray & Associates PLLC, having served previously as the acting Assistant Secretary for Policy at the U.S. Department of Labor. During his time there, he played a critical role in overseeing rulemaking and policy development. Berry also contributed to the nominations of Justice Neil Gorsuch and other federal judges. His career includes clerking for U.S. Supreme Court Justice Samuel Alito, making Berry a figure of significant influence in both labor policy and the federal judiciary.

Lindsey M. Burke is the Director of the Center for Education Policy at The Heritage Foundation. A key contributor to educational reform, she served on Virginia Governor Glenn Youngkin's education transition team and remains actively involved with various educational boards and institutions. Dr. Burke's work has been published in leading academic journals, solidifying her as an authoritative voice on education policy. Her academic journey includes degrees from Hollins University, the University of Virginia, and a PhD from George Mason University.

David R. Burton is a Senior Fellow in Economic Policy at The Heritage Foundation, focusing on securities regulation, tax policy, business law, and other areas. Burton's extensive career includes serving as General Counsel for the National Small Business Association, as well as leadership roles within the U.S. Chamber of Commerce. He holds degrees in law and economics, underscoring his expertise in U.S. financial and economic systems.

Adam Candeub, a professor of law at Michigan State University, is an expert in telecommunications, antitrust, and internet law. He has served in various government positions, including acting Assistant Secretary of Commerce during the Trump administration. Candeub's academic credentials from Yale University and the University of Pennsylvania position him as a distinguished voice in both legal and regulatory matters.

Dustin J. Carmack is a Research Fellow for Cybersecurity, Intelligence, and Emerging Technologies at The Heritage

Foundation. Carmack has worked closely with top intelligence officials, including serving as Chief of Staff to the Director of National Intelligence. His experience also extends to working with Congress, particularly with notable figures such as Congressman John Ratcliffe and Congressman Ron DeSantis.

Brendan Carr has extensive experience in communications and tech policy. Currently a senior Republican on the Federal Communications Commission (FCC), he previously served as the FCC's General Counsel and clerked for the U.S. Court of Appeals. Carr's educational background includes a law degree from the Catholic University of America.

Benjamin S. Carson, Sr., MD, widely known as Dr. Ben Carson, is a celebrated neurosurgeon and former Secretary of the U.S. Department of Housing and Urban Development. He founded the American Cornerstone Institute and has a remarkable life story, rising from poverty in Detroit to become a leading figure in medicine and politics. Dr. Carson's educational background includes degrees from Yale and the University of Michigan Medical School.

Ken Cuccinelli served as the Acting Director of U.S. Citizenship and Immigration Services and Acting Deputy Secretary of the U.S. Department of Homeland Security during the Trump administration. A former Attorney General of Virginia, Cuccinelli's career has been marked by leadership in immigration and regulatory policy.

Rick Dearborn is a political strategist and former Deputy Chief of Staff for President Donald Trump. Dearborn played a critical role in the 2016 presidential transition and held various senior roles in Senator Jeff Sessions' office. His previous work also includes positions at the U.S. Department of Energy and extensive experience in Republican politics.

Veronique de Rugy is a Senior Research Fellow at the Mercatus Center at George Mason University and a prominent economist. Her work focuses on the U.S. economy, federal budgets, and taxation. De Rugy writes regularly for major publications, including Reason magazine and the National Review Online, and holds a PhD in economics from the Panthéon-Sorbonne University in Paris.

Donald Devine, a Senior Scholar at The Fund for American Studies, was a key figure during the Reagan administration, where he led the Office of Personnel Management. His work on reducing bureaucracy earned him the title of "Reagan's Terrible Swift Sword of the Civil Service" by The Washington Post. Devine is also an author of ten books on political and economic matters.

Diana Furchtgott-Roth directs the Center for Energy, Climate, and Environment at The Heritage Foundation and teaches economics at George Washington University. She has served in senior roles under Presidents Ronald Reagan, George H.W. Bush, and George W. Bush. An Oxford-educated economist, her areas of expertise include energy policy and government research budgets.

Thomas F. Gilman held the position of Assistant Secretary of Commerce during the Trump administration. Gilman has spent over 40 years in the global automotive industry, including as CEO of Chrysler Financial. He also serves on several boards and has a strong background in corporate finance.

Mandy M. Gunasekara is a policy analyst and strategist specializing in energy and environmental issues. During the Trump administration, she served as Chief of Staff at the U.S. Environmental Protection Agency. Gunasekara also held various roles in the U.S. Congress, where she worked on energy policy.

Gene Hamilton is Vice President and General Counsel of America First Legal Foundation. Hamilton served in various capacities within the U.S. Department of Justice and Department of Homeland Security during the Trump administration. He has a legal background from Washington and Lee University and the University of Georgia.

Jennifer Hazelton is a communications expert with senior roles at the Department of Defense, USAID, and the State Department. Hazelton has also worked as a journalist for CNN and Fox News, bringing her extensive media expertise to her political consulting work.

Karen Kerrigan is the President and CEO of the Small Business & Entrepreneurship Council. She has worked for nearly three decades to promote entrepreneurship and small business growth in the U.S. and internationally. Kerrigan frequently testifies before Congress on issues impacting small businesses.

Dennis Dean Kirk is an experienced attorney who served in senior positions at the U.S. Office of Personnel Management during the Trump administration. He has received numerous awards for his work in the public sector and has a legal background that includes service with the U.S. Army's Office of General Counsel.

Kent Lassman is the President and CEO of the Competitive Enterprise Institute. Lassman's work focuses on telecommunications, privacy, and environmental regulations. He has worked across numerous state capitals and countries to advocate for free-market policies.

Bernard L. McNamee is a former member of the Federal Energy Regulatory Commission and an expert in energy law and regulation. He has held senior positions at the U.S. Department of Energy and worked for prominent political figures such as U.S. Senator Ted Cruz.

Christopher Miller, a former Acting U.S. Secretary of Defense, has served in multiple high-level roles in the Department of Defense and National Security Council. Miller has a distinguished military career as an Army Green Beret, with multiple combat tours in Iraq and Afghanistan.

Stephen Moore is a conservative economist and senior fellow at FreedomWorks and The Heritage Foundation. Moore has a long-standing career as an economics writer for The Wall Street Journal and remains a prominent voice in economic policy discussions.

Mora Namdar is an attorney and senior fellow at the American Foreign Policy Council, specializing in national security and international law. She served in various roles at the U.S. State Department during the Trump administration, focusing on human rights and global communications.

Peter Navarro, a former White House trade adviser under President Trump, played a key role in shaping U.S. trade policy with China. Navarro has written several books on U.S.-China relations and remains an influential voice in economic and trade matters.

William Perry Pendley is a lawyer and author who served as the acting director of the Bureau of Land Management during the Trump administration. Pendley has spent decades advocating for property rights and has argued several cases before the U.S. Supreme Court.

Max Primorac is the Director of the Douglas and Sarah Allison Center for Foreign Policy Studies at The Heritage Foundation. He has held significant roles, including acting Chief Operating Officer at the U.S. Agency for International Development's Bureau for Humanitarian Assistance and deputy director of Iraq's reconstruction program at the U.S. Department of State. Primorac is a graduate of Franklin and Marshall College and the University of Chicago.

Roger Severino serves as Vice President of Domestic Policy at The Heritage Foundation. He previously directed the Office for Civil Rights at the U.S. Department of Health and Human Services from 2017 to 2021, leading efforts in civil rights enforcement. Severino holds a JD from Harvard Law School, an MA in public policy from Carnegie Mellon University, and a BA from the University of Southern California.

Kiron K. Skinner is a renowned academic and policy expert, currently serving as President and CEO of the Foundation for America and the World. She has held prominent positions, including Director of Policy Planning at the U.S. Department of State and a fellowship at the Hoover Institution. Skinner holds an MA and PhD from Harvard University, with undergraduate degrees from Spelman College and Sacramento City College.

Brooks D. Tucker is a retired Marine lieutenant colonel and former Assistant Secretary for Congressional and Legislative Affairs at the U.S. Department of Veterans Affairs. He was instrumental in shaping national security and veterans' policy during his time with Senator Richard Burr and also served in Afghanistan, Iraq, and other regions. Tucker is a graduate of the University of Maryland and Georgetown University.

Hans A. von Spakovsky is a Senior Legal Fellow at The Heritage Foundation and manages the Election Law Reform Initiative. He served as a commissioner on the Federal Election Commission and was a member of President Trump's Advisory Commission on Election Integrity. Spakovsky also worked in the U.S. Department of Justice's Civil Rights Division.

Russ Vought is the founder and president of the Center for Renewing America and served as Director of the Office of Management and Budget under President Trump. He played a key role in implementing presidential budget policies and led efforts against critical race theory in federal agencies. Vought holds a JD from George Washington University Law School and a BA from Wheaton College.

William L. Walton is the Chairman of the Resolute Protector Foundation and host of The Bill Walton Show. He served on President Trump's transition team and was CEO of Allied Capital Corporation. Walton has been involved with several conservative organizations, including The Heritage Foundation and the American Conservative Union.

Paul Winfree is a Distinguished Fellow in Economic Policy at The Heritage Foundation. He held senior roles in the White House, including Deputy Director of the Domestic Policy Council, and played a key role during President Trump's transition. Winfree holds leadership positions in the Fulbright Foreign Scholarship Board.

AIMS AND PLANS OF THE PROJECT 2025

At the core of the conservative agenda outlined in "The Conservative Promise" are four broad fronts that will determine America's future:

- Restoring the Family as the Centerpiece of American Life and Protecting Our Children: The next conservative president must prioritize the well-being of the American family. The decline of the family unit is at the heart of many of the country's most pressing problems, from poverty to crime to mental health issues. Forty percent of all children in the United States are born to unmarried mothers, and in some communities, this number is even higher. The absence of fathers is one of the principal causes of poverty, crime, and a host of social ills. Government programs, while well-intentioned, cannot replace the role of a father or the stability of a married family. The next conservative administration must implement policies that promote family formation and stability, eliminate marriage penalties in federal welfare programs and the tax code, and install work requirements for government assistance programs like food stamps. Furthermore, federal power should be used to protect American children from the toxic influences of progressive ideologies, including the sexualization of children through transgender ideology and pornography.

- Dismantling the Administrative State and Returning Self-Governance to the American People: Over the past several decades, the growth of the administrative state has eroded individual freedoms and undermined the principle of self-governance. Federal agencies have amassed enormous power, often operating outside the oversight of Congress or the American people. The next conservative president must take steps to dismantle the administrative state and restore power to the people. This includes eliminating burdensome regulations, reducing the size of federal agencies, and holding unelected bureaucrats accountable. The goal is to return decision-making power to the states and local communities, where it rightfully belongs, and to ensure that the federal government serves the interests of the American people, not the other way around.
- Defending the Nation's Sovereignty, Borders, and Bounty Against Global Threats: America's sovereignty is under threat from both foreign adversaries and globalist elites. The rise of Communist China presents a significant challenge to America's economic and strategic interests. At the same time, open borders and illegal immigration have strained the nation's resources and undermined national security. The next conservative administration must take decisive action to secure the nation's borders, strengthen immigration enforcement, and protect American workers from unfair competition. Additionally, America's natural resources and economic bounty must be

safeguarded from global exploitation, ensuring that future generations can prosper.

- Securing God-Given Individual Rights to Live Freely: At the heart of the conservative agenda is the protection of individual rights and freedoms, as enshrined in the Constitution. These include the right to life, religious liberty, free speech, and the right to bear arms. In recent years, progressive elites have sought to undermine these rights through policies that infringe on religious freedom, promote censorship, and restrict Second Amendment rights. The next conservative president must stand firm in defending these God-given rights and work to undo the damage caused by years of progressive overreach. This includes enacting policies that protect the unborn, preserve religious liberty, and ensure that Americans can live freely without fear of government intrusion.

The key to the success of this conservative agenda lies in its ability to cut through the superficial distractions of modern politics and focus on the core moral and foundational challenges facing America today. This strategic clarity was one of the secrets of the Reagan Revolution's success, and it is a lesson that the current generation of conservatives must emulate. In the late 1970s, the political and cultural elites of the time had failed the American people, just as they have today. But conservatives found a way to unify, develop a clear plan, and lead the country out of decline. The threats of the past—socialism, the Soviet Union, and cultural deviancy— were defeated through strong leadership and bold action. Today, America faces new threats, but the conservative movement is once again prepared to rise to the occasion.

The next conservative president will face a range of challenges, but "The Conservative Promise" provides a clear roadmap for addressing these issues and restoring America to greatness. Whether it's defending the family, dismantling the administrative state, securing the nation's borders, or protecting individual freedoms, the conservative movement is ready to take bold action and lead the country through the current crisis.

The Heritage Foundation and its many partners have worked tirelessly to prepare for this moment. Project 2025 is about more than just winning the next election—it's about ensuring that the next conservative administration is ready on day one to govern effectively, implement conservative policies, and secure America's future. Just as the Mandate for Leadership helped to shape the Reagan presidency and bring about a conservative renaissance, "The Conservative Promise" aims to do the same for the next generation of conservative leaders. Victory is not guaranteed, but with a clear plan, strong leadership, and unity of purpose, conservatives can once again lead America out of decline and into a new era of prosperity, freedom, and human flourishing.

CHAPTER 1: A VISION FOR A CONSERVATIVE GOVERNMENT

1.1 OVERVIEW OF CONSERVATIVE GOVERNANCE

The conservative vision for governance centers on returning to the principles of limited government, decentralization, and the promotion of privatization. These guiding values emerge from a belief that a leaner government, with fewer bureaucratic controls, allows for a more effective and prosperous society. Conservatives argue that by minimizing federal power and restoring more authority to states and local governments, the country can better address the diverse needs of its citizens.

Historically, American governance was grounded in a system where states wielded considerable authority, with the federal government playing a narrower role in national defense, foreign policy, and ensuring the protection of individual rights. Over time, the federal government expanded its reach, particularly through the establishment of welfare programs, regulatory agencies, and other federal initiatives, which conservatives believe has undermined both the power and effectiveness of state governments. This shift, according to conservative thinkers, has led to an increasingly centralized state that struggles to meet the nuanced demands of a diverse population, further burdening the economy and taxpayers with excessive regulation and government intervention.

A core element of conservative governance is fiscal responsibility. Conservatives assert that the federal government's role should be primarily to create conditions for economic growth and stability, rather than acting as a large-scale provider of services. A key mechanism for achieving this is by reducing the federal bureaucracy, which is viewed as inefficient, slow-moving, and disconnected from the average citizen's needs. By slashing the size of the federal workforce and cutting down on unnecessary departments, agencies, and regulatory bodies, conservatives believe that governance can be streamlined, allowing the private sector to play a larger role in driving innovation, job creation, and economic development.

Decentralization is another critical aspect of the conservative governance model. In this vision, power is devolved from the federal government to state and local levels. The rationale behind this is that local governments are better positioned to understand the unique needs of their communities and can address issues more effectively than distant federal agencies. Decentralization allows for more experimentation in public policy, where states can serve as "laboratories of democracy" by trying different approaches to health care, education, and social welfare, with successful policies potentially being adopted by other states.

Privatization of public services is a hallmark of conservative policy, grounded in the belief that the private sector is generally more efficient and innovative than government-run programs. The conservative approach emphasizes competition as a means to improve quality and lower costs in sectors traditionally dominated by government, such as education, transportation, and healthcare. By reducing the federal government's direct involvement in these areas and allowing private enterprises to take the lead, conservatives argue that citizens will have access to better services, with more choice and accountability.

Another core principle of conservative governance is the protection of individual liberties, particularly in the face of expanding government oversight and control. Conservatives stress that a bloated federal government often encroaches on individual freedoms, whether through excessive taxation, regulation, or surveillance. In response, they advocate for stronger constitutional protections, particularly regarding freedom of speech, religion, and the right to bear arms. These protections, according to conservatives, are critical to ensuring that citizens retain autonomy over their lives and are not unduly constrained by government authority.

One of the biggest challenges conservatives identify in modern governance is the "deep state" or entrenched federal bureaucracy, which they see as resistant to reform and overly aligned with progressive, big-government ideals. Reforming or reducing the size of this bureaucratic apparatus is central to the conservative vision, as it is believed to be key to restoring individual liberty and enabling a more dynamic, market-driven economy. Conservative governance would seek to weaken the influence of these bureaucrats and empower elected officials and political appointees to drive policy decisions more directly.

Conservative governance also emphasizes a strong rule of law and respect for the Constitution as written. This includes a strict interpretation of the Constitution, whereby the federal government's powers are limited to those explicitly granted by the document, with all other powers reserved for the states and the people. This approach often results in opposition to expansive federal programs and interventions that are not seen as constitutionally justified, such as large-scale welfare systems, environmental regulations, or federal mandates in education.

Ultimately, conservatives believe that the federal government's primary role should be to safeguard the nation's security, protect individual freedoms, and ensure a fair playing field for economic opportunity, rather than acting as a provider of services or a regulator of individual behavior. By refocusing the government on these limited roles and empowering states and local governments, conservatives argue that the country can achieve greater prosperity, personal freedom, and social stability.

1.2 THE ROLE OF THE EXECUTIVE OFFICE

In the conservative framework, the Executive Office of the President (EOP) plays a pivotal role in implementing the administration's policy agenda and steering the federal government toward reform. Strengthening the EOP is critical to executing the vision of limited government, decentralization, and privatization.

The EOP serves as the President's principal administrative and advisory body, ensuring that the policies of the administration are effectively carried out across the federal government. To achieve the conservative goal of reducing bureaucracy and federal intervention, the EOP must be robust, well-organized, and composed of individuals who are firmly aligned with conservative values. The personnel choices within the EOP are critical, as the adage "personnel is policy" underscores. The conservative movement views the appointment of officials who adhere to the principles of limited government, free-market economics, and individual liberty as essential to achieving the administration's broader policy objectives.

One of the central functions of the EOP in a conservative administration is to act as a force for accountability and efficiency within the federal government. The EOP's leadership must ensure that federal agencies operate within their constitutional mandates, avoiding mission creep and regulatory overreach. The Office of Management and Budget (OMB) plays a crucial role in this effort, overseeing the federal budget and working to eliminate wasteful spending and programs that exceed the government's core responsibilities.

Moreover, the EOP must be structured in a way that enables the President to maintain direct control over key aspects of governance. A strong Chief of Staff is vital in this context, serving as the President's top aide and overseeing the coordination of the White House's various offices. The Chief of Staff ensures that all departments within the EOP are aligned with the President's vision and are working cohesively to implement it.

The EOP also houses the National Security Council (NSC), which is integral to guiding foreign and defense policy. In a conservative administration, the NSC would focus on strengthening national sovereignty, securing borders, and maintaining a strong national defense, while being cautious about foreign entanglements. This aligns with the conservative view that America should be a leader on the world stage without engaging in unnecessary interventions or nation-building efforts abroad. The NSC must work closely with the Department of Defense, the Department of State, and intelligence agencies to implement a foreign policy that prioritizes America's national interests and security.

Conservatives also seek to ensure that the EOP fosters strong relationships with Congress, particularly with members who share conservative values. The Office of Legislative Affairs (OLA) is tasked with managing these relationships, working to advance the President's legislative agenda. The OLA coordinates with lawmakers to secure votes for key policy initiatives, including tax reform, deregulation, and efforts to reduce federal spending. In a conservative administration, the OLA plays an essential role in dismantling existing government programs that are deemed excessive, while promoting legislation that aligns with conservative principles of limited government and economic freedom.

Another vital component of the EOP is the Office of Communications, which manages the administration's public messaging. In the conservative vision, effective communication is key to gaining public support for reforms that may face opposition from entrenched interests, both within and outside of government. The Communications Office ensures that the President's message is clear, cohesive, and resonates with the values of the American people. Whether addressing the media, Congress, or the public, the administration must communicate its commitment to restoring limited government, protecting individual freedoms, and promoting economic opportunity.

The conservative approach to governance places a premium on the integrity and competence of White House staff. Presidential appointees, including those within the EOP, are expected to adhere strictly to ethical standards, ensuring that the administration operates transparently and efficiently. By selecting individuals who are ideologically aligned and competent in their roles, the administration can ensure that its policy agenda is implemented effectively and without bureaucratic obstruction.

Additionally, the EOP plays a key role in nominating federal judges and Supreme Court justices who interpret the Constitution in line with originalist and textualist principles. This judicial philosophy is central to the conservative vision, as it seeks to prevent the expansion of federal power through judicial activism. By appointing judges who adhere to a strict interpretation of the Constitution, the President can ensure that conservative values are upheld in the judiciary, safeguarding individual liberties and limiting the government's ability to overreach.

Finally, the EOP must work to ensure that federal agencies are staffed with individuals who are not only competent but also dedicated to implementing the administration's policy agenda. The Office of Presidential Personnel (PPO) is responsible for identifying, vetting, and appointing individuals to key positions throughout the executive branch. In a conservative administration, the PPO's work is crucial for ensuring that political appointees are not undermined by career bureaucrats who may resist change or seek to obstruct conservative reforms.

CHAPTER 2: REFORMING THE EXECUTIVE BRANCH

2.1 EXECUTIVE OFFICE OF THE PRESIDENT

The Executive Office of the President (EOP) plays a critical role in shaping and implementing the President's policies. To streamline governance and increase efficiency, conservative governance emphasizes the reorganization of key executive offices within the EOP. This is necessary to ensure that the President's agenda can be executed without interference from entrenched bureaucratic elements. The focus is on reducing redundancy, fostering accountability, and improving coordination between the White House and various executive agencies.

At the heart of this reorganization is the recognition that the executive branch, as it currently exists, has become a sprawling bureaucracy with an outsized influence on policymaking. Many career bureaucrats, rather than following the directives of elected officials, pursue their own agendas, often hindering the policy objectives of a new administration. As such, reforming the EOP involves reducing the power of career officials while ensuring that political appointees are empowered to drive policy implementation.

Reorganizing for Efficiency The EOP should be structured to ensure that the President's advisors and political appointees have the tools necessary to implement the President's agenda effectively. This includes revisiting the roles of various offices and determining where redundancies can be eliminated. Offices like the Domestic Policy Council, National Security Council, and National Economic Council are vital to ensuring that the administration's priorities are coordinated across the federal government, but they must operate efficiently and avoid overlap. A streamlined structure ensures that key initiatives, from national security to economic reform, are executed in a cohesive manner.

A critical aspect of reorganization is ensuring that the President's political appointees hold key decision-making positions within the EOP. These appointees must be aligned with the administration's conservative principles of limited government, free-market economics, and decentralization. The Office of Management and Budget (OMB), for example, must be led by individuals who are committed to fiscal responsibility and cutting unnecessary spending across federal agencies.

The Role of the Office of Management and Budget (OMB) The OMB is one of the most important offices within the EOP when it comes to executing the President's policy agenda. The OMB serves as the President's air traffic control system, ensuring that all policy initiatives are in sync and that the bureaucracy is following the administration's directives. It has several key responsibilities, including:

Developing and enforcing the President's budget.

Managing agency performance, procurement, and financial management.

Developing the President's regulatory agenda.

Reviewing regulatory actions and setting information policy.

The OMB plays a critical role in ensuring that the federal government adheres to fiscal discipline. Through the budget process, the OMB ensures that the administration's priorities are funded while also cutting wasteful programs and enforcing budget neutrality across agencies. One tool to achieve this is the concept of administrative "pay-as-you-go" (PAYGO), which requires agencies to offset any discretionary spending increases with cuts elsewhere. This simple procedural requirement forces agencies to exercise fiscal responsibility.

The OMB also plays a crucial role in the regulatory process. It is responsible for reviewing proposed regulations from federal agencies to ensure that they align with the administration's goals of deregulation and reducing the burden on businesses and individuals. By having political appointees lead this process, the OMB can ensure that regulations do not stifle economic growth or encroach on individual liberties.

The OMB's management portfolio includes offices like the Office of Federal Procurement Policy, which sets contracting rules for the federal government, and the Office of Information and Regulatory Affairs, which reviews regulatory actions. These offices are essential for driving policy changes that reflect the President's vision for a more efficient and accountable federal government.

2.2 THE VICE PRESIDENT'S OFFICE

The role of the Vice President has evolved significantly over the years, becoming an increasingly integral part of the administration. While the Vice President has always held important constitutional responsibilities—such as serving as President of the Senate and breaking tie votes—modern Vice Presidents have taken on a much more active role in shaping and executing presidential policies.

A Key Adviser to the President The Vice President is often one of the President's most trusted advisers, playing a key role in policy formation and execution. In recent administrations, the Vice President has been given office space in the West Wing, reflecting the importance of close proximity to the President and other senior advisers. This proximity allows the Vice President to be involved in daily decision-making and policy discussions, ensuring that they can effectively support the President's agenda.

The Vice President's office, like the EOP, should be staffed with individuals who are aligned with the administration's goals and capable of executing its policies. The Vice President is expected to have their own team of domestic policy and national security advisers who work in tandem with the President's team to ensure that the administration's priorities are advanced across all areas of governance.

Leading Key Initiatives In recent administrations', Vice Presidents have often been tasked with leading specific initiatives or policy areas. For example, Vice President Mike Pence was given responsibility for coordinating the federal response to the COVID-19 pandemic. Other Vice

Presidents have led efforts on space policy, deregulation, and workforce development. These assignments reflect the growing importance of the Vice President in executing the President's agenda.

The Vice President is also a statutory member of the National Security Council, which provides them with a direct role in shaping the administration's foreign and defense policies. In this capacity, the Vice President can offer unique insights and help ensure that the President's national security priorities are carried out effectively.

A Training Ground for the Presidency Historically, many Vice Presidents have gone on to become Presidents themselves, making the Vice Presidency a crucial training ground for the nation's highest office. By playing an active role in policy formation and implementation, Vice Presidents gain valuable experience that prepares them for the challenges of the presidency. This dynamic ensures that the Vice President is not only a key member of the current administration but also a potential future leader of the country.

Ambassadorial and Legislative Roles In addition to their domestic responsibilities, Vice Presidents often serve as ambassadors for the administration abroad, representing the United States in meetings with foreign leaders and promoting the administration's policies on the global stage. They also play a critical role in navigating the legislative process, particularly in the Senate, where they can cast tie-breaking votes and act as a liaison between the administration and Congress.

CHAPTER 3: NATIONAL SECURITY AND DEFENSE

3.1 DEPARTMENT OF DEFENSE (DOD)

Restructuring Defense Priorities

In this section, the vision for restructuring the Department of Defense (DOD) revolves around refocusing the U.S. military's priorities towards strategic defense rather than global policing. This change is meant to better align military expenditures and operational efforts with the core objectives of national defense, while limiting involvement in prolonged international conflicts that don't directly threaten U.S. national security. The conservative approach seeks to ensure that the U.S. military remains capable of defending the homeland while being prudent in how and where military resources are deployed.

Historically, the U.S. military has been involved in various global conflicts, often adopting a role of global enforcer and engaging in nation-building efforts. Such endeavors have frequently stretched the military thin and led to significant financial and human costs without necessarily enhancing U.S. security. Instead of engaging in international policing, the new priority under conservative leadership is to reduce the frequency of military interventions abroad, particularly those that do not serve a clear national security purpose.

Strategic Defense and Technological Investments

To meet this goal, a significant restructuring is proposed that emphasizes the modernization of the military's strategic defense systems. This involves a major investment in missile defense systems and hypersonic weapons development, which are seen as critical to deterring future threats from adversaries such as China, Russia, and rogue states like North Korea.

The Department of Defense will prioritize missile defense systems that can address both traditional ballistic missile threats and new advanced weapons, such as hypersonic missiles. Hypersonic missiles travel at extremely high speeds, making them difficult to intercept with current defense technologies. Investment in counter-hypersonic capabilities is therefore deemed essential. Key areas of focus include:

Missile Defense Systems: The U.S. military will accelerate the development and deployment of advanced missile defense technologies like the Next Generation Interceptor (NGI), which offers better protection than current systems like the Ground-Based Interceptor (GBI). Along with this, efforts will focus on layered missile defense systems, which offer multiple layers of protection against incoming threats. These systems will be essential for defending not only the U.S. homeland but also military assets and allies abroad.

Hypersonic Weapons Development: Hypersonic missile systems are another critical area of investment. As rival nations advance their own hypersonic missile capabilities, the U.S. must develop effective countermeasures. This includes investing in Glide Phase Interceptor (GPI) technology and space-based missile detection systems that can track and intercept hypersonic missiles. These developments are aimed at ensuring that the U.S. maintains a strategic edge in missile defense capabilities.

Technological Innovation: Beyond missile defense, broader technological innovations in areas like artificial intelligence (AI), cyber warfare, and autonomous systems are crucial for maintaining U.S. military dominance in a rapidly changing global security environment. The DOD will aim to modernize its acquisition process to ensure faster adoption of new technologies while eliminating outdated and ineffective programs. By streamlining procurement and testing processes, the DOD can more effectively respond to emerging threats.

Shifting Military Doctrine

The restructuring of the DOD also includes a shift in military doctrine. Instead of focusing on counterinsurgency operations and prolonged foreign interventions, the military will prepare for high-intensity conflicts against near-peer competitors. This involves reallocating resources to naval, air, and space forces, which are more suitable for deterring and defeating major state adversaries. Ground forces will remain essential but will be restructured to focus on rapid deployment and strategic strike capabilities rather than long-term occupation missions.

3.2 DEPARTMENT OF HOMELAND SECURITY (DHS)

Reforming Immigration Enforcement and Border Security

The Department of Homeland Security (DHS) plays a central role in protecting the U.S. from external threats, particularly through its responsibility for border security and immigration enforcement. The chapter emphasizes the need for significant reforms in these areas to restore control over the U.S. border and implement more effective immigration policies. The conservative approach calls for a robust enforcement mechanism that focuses on securing the border, detaining illegal entrants, and deporting those who are in the country unlawfully.

Border Security

One of the main priorities is regaining control of the U.S.-Mexico border, which has seen a surge in illegal crossings in recent years. Under conservative leadership, DHS will prioritize the construction and fortification of physical barriers, such as border walls, as a key measure to deter illegal immigration. Border security technology, including advanced surveillance systems, drones, and motion sensors, will be deployed to supplement physical barriers. These measures are designed to create a more secure and manageable border environment.

In addition to physical infrastructure, the reorganization of DHS will involve reallocating personnel and resources to improve enforcement at the border. U.S. Customs and Border Protection (CBP) and Immigration and Customs Enforcement (ICE) will be given more resources to carry out their missions effectively. This includes increasing the number of agents and officers tasked with border enforcement and immigration adjudication. By increasing manpower and infrastructure, DHS can respond more effectively to surges in illegal immigration and smuggling operations.

Immigration Enforcement

The restructuring of immigration enforcement will also involve consolidating the responsibilities of various immigration-related agencies to improve efficiency. For example, ICE, CBP, and the U.S. Citizenship and Immigration Services (USCIS) may be integrated into a more unified border and immigration agency. This would reduce bureaucratic overlap and create a more streamlined process for addressing both legal and illegal immigration cases.

A key reform will be restoring strict enforcement of immigration laws. Under the new approach, the use of deportation and detention will be ramped up to deter illegal immigration. Expedited removal processes, which allow for the quick deportation of illegal entrants, will be expanded. DHS will also work to end policies that allow for "catch and release," where individuals who are apprehended for illegal entry are released into the U.S. pending court hearings, often disappearing without a trace.

Furthermore, ICE will be tasked with a more aggressive posture in detaining and deporting individuals who pose a national security or public safety risk. This includes criminal aliens, individuals with prior deportation orders, and those involved in criminal enterprises such as human trafficking or drug smuggling.

Preventing Overreach in Intelligence Services

Another area of reform is the decentralization of intelligence services under DHS to prevent overreach and mission creep. The Cybersecurity and Infrastructure Security Agency (CISA), which has been criticized for expanding its role beyond its statutory responsibilities, will be reined in. CISA's focus will return to its core mission of protecting critical infrastructure and ensuring cybersecurity, rather than engaging in activities like content moderation or election influence operations.

Intelligence functions that do not directly align with DHS's core mission of securing the homeland will be transferred to other departments, such as the Department of Justice (DOJ) or the Department of Defense (DOD). This decentralization aims to reduce the risk of mission creep and ensure that intelligence resources are focused on addressing actual security threats, rather than engaging in politically motivated activities.

Reallocating Resources and Reducing Bureaucracy

DHS, like many other federal agencies, has grown into a massive bureaucracy since its creation following the 9/11 terrorist attacks. The department has been criticized for inefficiency, waste, and mission drift, particularly under administrations that have prioritized political or ideological objectives over national security. The chapter outlines plans to streamline DHS operations, eliminate unnecessary programs, and cut down on bureaucratic bloat.

One major proposal is the privatization of certain functions within DHS, such as the Transportation Security Administration (TSA). By outsourcing airport security to private companies, DHS can reduce operational costs while improving efficiency. Similarly, the Federal Emergency Management Agency (FEMA) may see some of its responsibilities, particularly those related to disaster recovery, devolved to state and local governments. This would shift the burden of emergency preparedness away from the federal government, aligning with the conservative philosophy of decentralization.

CHAPTER 4: ECONOMIC PROSPERITY

4.1 DEPARTMENT OF TREASURY

Promoting Tax Reforms to Stimulate Economic Growth

The Department of Treasury is pivotal in fostering a healthy economy, and conservative policy focuses on the need for fundamental tax reforms to stimulate economic growth. These reforms are aimed at incentivizing work, savings, investment, and entrepreneurship, all while minimizing the burden of taxation on individuals and businesses.

The core of conservative tax reform involves reducing marginal tax rates, broadening the tax base, and simplifying the tax code. The overarching goal is to create an environment where economic decisions are driven by market forces rather than tax considerations. By reducing marginal tax rates, individuals are encouraged to work more and invest in their future, as the returns on these efforts are higher. At the same time, reducing corporate tax rates makes the U.S. more competitive internationally, attracting investment and promoting job creation.

A simplified tax code, one with fewer deductions, credits, and exclusions, ensures that taxes are neutral and do not distort economic decision-making. Special-interest tax breaks are seen as inefficient and unfair, leading to economic distortions that harm long-term growth. Conservatives advocate for the elimination of these provisions to level the playing field and ensure that taxes do not disproportionately favor certain industries or individuals.

One key reform includes a two-tier individual tax system, with rates at 15% and 30%. This system eliminates most deductions and exclusions, simplifying compliance and reducing loopholes that wealthier taxpayers often exploit. The simplification also allows for greater transparency and fairness, ensuring that taxpayers are treated equally regardless of their income level.

In addition to individual tax reforms, corporate tax reductions are a major focus. The corporate tax rate would be reduced to 18%, a level that conservatives argue is essential for keeping the U.S. competitive in a global market. The burden of corporate taxation primarily falls on workers due to the mobility of capital, and lower rates would likely lead to higher wages and greater investment in the domestic economy. Immediate expensing of capital expenditures is also encouraged, enabling businesses to reinvest their profits more efficiently and spurring economic growth.

Moreover, capital gains and dividends are taxed at 15%, ensuring that the combined corporate income and personal income tax rates on investment returns are roughly equal to the top individual income tax rate. This structure is designed to encourage investment in capital markets without creating disproportionate tax burdens on business activities.

Encouraging Free Market Principles

The Treasury is tasked with fostering a free market environment by limiting government intervention and allowing market forces to allocate resources effectively. Free market policies emphasize reducing regulatory burdens that stifle business growth and innovation, as well as promoting tax competition among nations. Tax competition is seen as a mechanism to prevent governments from imposing overly burdensome tax rates, as businesses and individuals can relocate to jurisdictions with more favorable tax policies.

One proposal includes the introduction of Universal Savings Accounts (USAs). These accounts would allow individuals to save post-tax earnings up to $15,000 annually, with gains exempt from future taxation. USAs would give families greater flexibility in managing their finances, whether for retirement, education, or emergency expenses, without facing double taxation on their savings.

To further promote entrepreneurship, conservatives advocate increasing the business loss limitation to $500,000 and allowing companies to carry forward net operating losses. Reducing extra layers of taxes on capital, such as the net investment income surtax and the base erosion anti-abuse tax, would provide additional incentives for businesses to expand and innovate. Moreover, the estate and gift tax should be reduced to no higher than 20%, ensuring that family-owned businesses and farms can be passed down without facing significant tax penalties.

In terms of energy and trade, the Treasury must reverse policies that support international public efforts promoting Environmental, Social, and Governance (ESG) standards. These policies are perceived as undermining U.S. energy security by discouraging investment in traditional energy sectors like oil and gas. Instead, the focus should be on promoting investment in domestic energy production to secure long-term prosperity.

4.2 FEDERAL TRADE COMMISSION (FTC)

Conservative Approaches to Antitrust and Market Regulation

The Federal Trade Commission (FTC) was established to enforce antitrust laws and prevent unfair competition, ensuring a competitive marketplace that benefits consumers. However, modern conservative thought argues that antitrust regulation must be limited to situations where consumer welfare is demonstrably harmed. The central tenet of this approach is that a competitive economy maximizes both allocative efficiency (the optimal distribution of goods and services) and productive efficiency (the least use of resources for maximum output), ultimately improving consumer welfare.

Historically, antitrust laws like the Sherman Act (1890) and the Clayton Act (1914) were enacted to break up monopolies and prevent anti-competitive practices. However, conservative economists, most notably Robert Bork, have argued that antitrust enforcement has often been misapplied in ways that harm consumers by protecting smaller competitors at the expense of efficiency. Bork's influential work, "The Antitrust Paradox," emphasized that the primary goal of antitrust law should be to ensure consumer welfare, rather than simply preventing large companies from gaining market share.

Under this view, market size and concentration are not inherently bad. As long as companies achieve their dominance through legitimate competition—offering better products at lower prices—they should not be penalized. For instance, vertical mergers or exclusive dealing agreements that may seem anti-competitive on the surface could, in fact, result in greater efficiencies and lower prices for consumers. Antitrust laws should not be used to artificially constrain corporate growth or innovation unless there is clear evidence of consumer harm, such as price-fixing or predatory pricing.

The Role of the FTC in Consumer Protection

While the FTC's mandate includes protecting consumers from unfair business practices, conservatives argue that markets, not the government, are the best mechanism for delivering what consumers want. Government intervention should be minimal, as markets are self-regulating and dynamic, capable of addressing consumer needs more efficiently than bureaucratic oversight.

However, there are growing concerns about the role of Big Tech and other large corporations in the modern economy, especially in their influence over political discourse and social institutions. Some conservatives argue that concentrated economic power can lead to abuses that go beyond pricing and efficiency concerns. For example, large internet platforms may use their dominance to suppress free speech or impose political agendas on their users. This complicates the traditional consumer welfare standard, as it raises questions about the role of corporations in shaping democratic institutions and civil society.

In response, there is a call within conservative circles for the FTC to adapt its enforcement standards to account for these broader issues, including the influence of large firms on free speech and market entry barriers for new competitors. This recalibration would not involve a return to aggressive antitrust enforcement but would instead ensure that large corporations do not collude with government agencies or stifle innovation in ways that harm the broader economy and democracy.

Consumer Welfare and Free Markets

Conservative economic policy emphasizes the importance of free markets in promoting consumer welfare. When markets are competitive, businesses are forced to innovate, improve their products, and lower prices to attract customers. This competition ensures that consumers benefit from better products and services at lower costs. Government intervention, on the other hand, often leads to unintended consequences, such as higher costs and reduced consumer choice.

One area where conservatives see a need for government intervention is in the regulatory burden placed on small businesses. The cost of complying with federal regulations disproportionately affects smaller firms, as they lack the resources to navigate complex regulatory frameworks. By contrast, larger companies can absorb these costs more easily, which gives them a competitive advantage. The FTC must consider the role of government regulation in fostering market concentration and work to reduce these barriers to entry for smaller firms.

In conclusion, both the Treasury Department and the FTC play critical roles in fostering economic growth and ensuring that markets remain competitive. Conservative approaches to these institutions emphasize minimizing government intervention, promoting tax reforms that encourage investment and entrepreneurship, and ensuring that antitrust laws protect consumer welfare without stifling innovation or market efficiency. By focusing on these principles, the next administration aims to create a prosperous, free-market economy that benefits all Americans.

CHAPTER 5: ENERGY INDEPENDENCE

5.1 DEPARTMENT OF ENERGY (DOE)

Reversing the Current Administration's Policies on Renewable Energy

The current conservative vision for the Department of Energy (DOE) advocates a departure from policies focused predominantly on renewable energy, particularly the aggressive pursuit of net-zero carbon emissions. Under the Biden administration, the DOE has prioritized the decarbonization of the economy, largely sidelining fossil fuel industries in favor of renewable resources like wind, solar, and sustainable transportation. Conservatives argue that this approach has skewed the energy market by heavily subsidizing renewables at the expense of more reliable energy sources, such as oil, gas, and coal.

The new conservative direction emphasizes the need to shift focus back to energy security and the affordability of energy for American consumers. The DOE would reduce its commitment to decarbonization efforts and instead refocus on ensuring energy reliability, affordability, and security through a diverse energy portfolio that includes fossil fuels. This strategy involves eliminating government programs that promote renewable energy commercialization and scaling back taxpayer-funded initiatives that benefit green industries at the expense of the broader economy.

Promoting Fossil Fuel Development to Restore Energy Independence

The core of the energy independence agenda is to revive fossil fuel development, which conservatives argue is vital for the country's energy security and economic growth. By investing in the domestic production of oil, natural gas, and coal, the U.S. can reduce its dependence on foreign energy supplies, particularly from adversarial nations. A robust fossil fuel industry also creates jobs and ensures the availability of affordable energy, which is crucial for the economic well-being of the American people.

Conservatives propose renaming and restructuring the Office of Fossil Energy and Carbon Management (FECM) back to its original purpose: increasing energy security and supply through fossil fuels. This would eliminate unnecessary programs focused on carbon management and decarbonization, instead channeling resources into enhancing fossil fuel efficiency and reducing environmental impacts through technological innovation.

A significant aspect of this strategy is to expedite the approval process for liquefied natural gas (LNG) exports. The current lengthy regulatory procedures slow down the export of American LNG, a resource that could play a key role in stabilizing global energy markets and reducing reliance on Russian and Middle Eastern gas. Expedited approvals and expanded automatic approvals for LNG exports to allies and free trade partners would bolster both American economic interests and global energy security.

Another critical component of the strategy is the proper use of the Strategic Petroleum Reserve (SPR). Conservatives argue that the SPR should be maintained for genuine national security emergencies, not used for political purposes to manipulate energy markets. Misuse of the SPR, such as for artificially reducing gas prices ahead of elections, undermines its role as a national safeguard.

Balancing Environmental Concerns with Energy Security

While environmental stewardship remains important, the conservative perspective emphasizes that environmental regulations should not come at the expense of energy reliability or economic prosperity. The DOE would pivot from policies that focus on aggressive carbon reduction targets to policies that balance energy production with responsible environmental practices. This approach would not dismiss renewable energy outright but would place it within a broader energy strategy that includes all viable resources, particularly fossil fuels, as essential to maintaining energy security.

5.2 ENVIRONMENTAL PROTECTION AGENCY (EPA)

Reducing the Regulatory Burden of Environmental Policies

The Environmental Protection Agency (EPA) has been a focal point of conservative criticism, particularly regarding its role in advancing climate-focused policies that conservatives argue overreach the agency's statutory authority. Since the Obama administration, and further during the Biden administration, the EPA has been used as a tool to pursue expansive environmental goals, often without the backing of Congress. These policies have imposed significant costs on the economy, particularly in the energy and manufacturing sectors, through stringent environmental regulations.

The conservative agenda calls for reducing the regulatory burden imposed by the EPA, particularly in industries like energy, agriculture, and manufacturing. The goal is to restore the EPA's focus on its core mission: protecting air and water quality without engaging in overregulation that stifles economic growth. This would involve significant reforms aimed at scaling back the EPA's authority in areas like carbon emissions and energy production, where regulations have been used to phase out fossil fuels in favor of renewables.

One proposed reform is to end the EPA's focus on global climate change efforts, which have driven policies that conservatives believe are detrimental to U.S. economic interests. By prioritizing climate change as a central issue, the EPA has implemented regulations that favor renewable energy and restrict traditional energy industries, particularly coal and oil. These policies have led to job losses in energy-producing regions and increased energy costs for consumers.

Conservatives argue that environmental regulation should be grounded in tangible, measurable improvements to public health and the environment, not in abstract goals like reducing global temperatures. Therefore, the EPA's regulatory scope should be narrowed to address specific environmental concerns, such as reducing pollution in a cost-effective and practical manner, rather than imposing blanket mandates that result in economic hardship.

Aligning the EPA's Mission with Economic Growth and Less Activism

Another core tenet of the conservative reform agenda is to reorient the EPA away from activist-driven environmental policies that prioritize ideological goals over economic realities. The agency's mission should be aligned with fostering economic growth while ensuring reasonable environmental protections. This would involve promoting cooperative federalism, where state and local governments take a leading role in setting and enforcing environmental standards that reflect the specific needs of their communities. The EPA would shift to a more supportive role, providing expertise and resources to states rather than imposing one-size-fits-all mandates from the federal level.

This approach also involves streamlining the EPA's processes to eliminate unnecessary, duplicative, or superfluous programs. Many of the current regulations, particularly those introduced under the Biden administration, are viewed as overreaching and not cost-beneficial. By reducing the complexity and scope of these regulations, the EPA would create a more predictable regulatory environment that encourages investment in energy production and industrial development.

A key area of focus for reform is the Clean Air Act (CAA) and the Clean Water Act (CWA). Both laws have been used in recent years to implement far-reaching regulations that conservatives argue go beyond their original intent. For example, the expansion of air quality regulations under the CAA has imposed costly requirements on power plants and factories, many of which are located in economically disadvantaged regions. By rolling back these expansions, conservatives aim to protect industries from burdensome regulations while maintaining reasonable standards for environmental protection.

Restoring Trust in the EPA through Transparency and Accountability

One of the long-standing critiques of the EPA is its perceived lack of transparency and accountability, particularly in how it uses science to justify regulatory actions. Conservatives argue that the EPA has often relied on opaque or biased scientific studies to support sweeping regulations that have far-reaching economic impacts. To address this, the conservative agenda calls for increased transparency in the EPA's decision-making process. This includes making all scientific data and studies used in regulatory decisions publicly available for scrutiny and ensuring that regulatory actions are based on sound, peer-reviewed science.

Moreover, the EPA would shift its enforcement focus from punitive actions to cooperative compliance. Instead of aggressively fining businesses for violations, the agency would work more closely with industries to help them meet environmental standards in a cost-effective manner. This cooperative approach aims to reduce the adversarial relationship between the EPA and the private sector, fostering a regulatory environment where compliance is encouraged, not coerced.

Conclusion

Chapter 5 outlines a fundamental shift in energy and environmental policy under a conservative administration. The DOE's role would be reoriented toward promoting fossil fuel development to achieve energy independence, while renewable energy would be placed in a supporting role rather than being the central focus. The EPA, meanwhile, would see its regulatory scope reduced, with a focus on transparency, accountability, and aligning its mission with economic growth. By prioritizing energy security, reducing regulatory burdens, and restoring trust in environmental governance, conservatives aim to create a balanced approach that ensures both environmental stewardship and economic prosperity

CHAPTER 6: STRENGTHENING AGRICULTURE

6.1 DEPARTMENT OF AGRICULTURE (USDA)

Reforming Subsidies and Reducing the Influence of Environmental Groups on Farming Policy

The U.S. Department of Agriculture (USDA) plays a critical role in American agriculture, with an extensive history of involvement in both supporting farmers and regulating agricultural practices. A key focus of conservative reform is the restructuring of farm subsidies and reducing the influence of environmental groups on agricultural policy. The conservative vision seeks to balance providing a safety net for farmers with the need to avoid distorting markets or encouraging overdependence on government aid.

Reforming Agricultural Subsidies

Agricultural subsidies have long been a contentious issue in U.S. farming policy. Programs such as the Agriculture Risk Coverage (ARC) and Price Loss Coverage (PLC) are designed to shield farmers from market fluctuations by offering financial support when prices or revenues fall below a certain threshold. Additionally, the federal crop insurance program is widely used to provide protection against losses in revenue or crop yields. However, these programs have created unintended market distortions and inefficiencies. For instance, the ARC and PLC programs have been criticized for encouraging overproduction by reducing the risks associated with price volatility.

Conservative reform advocates argue that the federal government's involvement in subsidies should be minimized to foster a more market-driven agricultural economy. One proposal is to repeal the ARC and PLC programs entirely, relying instead on the federal crop insurance program to provide necessary support. Critics of ARC, in particular, argue that it encourages "shallow loss" protection, which compensates farmers for minor revenue losses that do not constitute genuine hardship. Eliminating or reducing such programs would help realign agricultural policy with the principles of risk management and market efficiency.

Another area of reform focuses on reducing the overlap between subsidy programs. Currently, farmers can receive payments from both ARC or PLC programs and the federal crop insurance program, effectively "double-dipping" on government aid. To address this, reform proposals suggest prohibiting farmers from receiving both types of payments in the same year. By streamlining subsidy programs and eliminating redundancy, the USDA can ensure that financial assistance is targeted toward those who truly need it, without inflating costs to taxpayers.

Beyond ARC and PLC, the federal sugar program has long been a target for conservative reformers. The program restricts the domestic supply of sugar to drive up prices, benefiting a small number of sugar producers while costing consumers billions of dollars annually. Repealing the sugar program is viewed as an essential step toward reducing government intervention in agriculture and restoring free-market principles.

Conservatives argue that reforming subsidies will also reduce the distortionary effects these programs have on environmental practices. Current subsidies can incentivize farming on marginal lands, which are often environmentally sensitive. Eliminating or reducing subsidies for overproduction will help ensure that farming practices align more closely with environmental stewardship goals.

Reducing the Influence of Environmental Groups on Farming Policy

Conservative reformers also emphasize the need to reduce the influence of environmental groups on USDA policy. In recent years, the USDA has increasingly aligned its policies with broader environmental and climate goals, particularly under the Biden administration. For example, initiatives like "climate-smart" agriculture, which prioritize reducing carbon emissions and mitigating climate change, have taken precedence over more traditional concerns, such as maximizing food production and supporting farmers.

The conservative perspective views this shift as an overreach that prioritizes environmental activism over the practical needs of American farmers. Conservatives argue that while environmental protection is important, the USDA's primary mission should be to support agricultural productivity and food security. Programs that impose restrictive environmental regulations, such as limits on pesticide use or mandates for organic farming, are seen as costly and counterproductive, especially when they do not account for the practical realities of farming.

For example, the USDA's push for organic farming, which includes financial incentives for farmers to transition to organic practices, has been criticized for ignoring the economic realities of organic farming, which is typically more labor-intensive and yields lower output than conventional farming. Critics argue that farmers are better positioned than policymakers to make decisions about the best farming practices for their land.

To address this, conservative reforms advocate for removing or limiting USDA programs that focus on climate change and environmental activism. Instead, the USDA should focus on ensuring that farmers have the tools and resources they need to meet growing food demand. This includes rolling back regulations that impose unnecessary costs on farmers, such as burdensome environmental reviews or mandates for certain types of conservation practices. By reducing the regulatory burden on farmers, the USDA can help to create an environment where agricultural innovation can thrive, leading to greater productivity and sustainability.

Ensuring that the USDA Respects the Role of American Farmers Without Excessive Government Interference

A key principle of conservative agricultural policy is the belief that the government should respect the autonomy of American farmers. Farmers, according to this view, are best equipped to make decisions about how to manage their land, grow their crops, and run their operations. Excessive government intervention, whether through overregulation or centrally planned agricultural policies, is seen as a threat to the independence and productivity of American agriculture.

To this end, conservative reforms call for reducing the scope of the USDA's authority and returning more decision-making power to farmers and local communities. One proposal is to decentralize certain regulatory functions and delegate more responsibility to state and local governments. This approach is based on the principle of cooperative federalism, where the federal government sets broad goals but allows states and localities to implement regulations in a way that reflects the unique needs and conditions of their agricultural regions.

Additionally, there is a push to streamline the USDA's operations and reduce bureaucratic inefficiencies that can hinder farmers' ability to innovate and respond to market changes. This includes eliminating unnecessary programs and cutting back on the USDA's involvement in areas that fall outside its core mission of supporting agricultural productivity. For instance, the USDA currently administers a wide range of programs related to rural development, food security, and environmental conservation, many of which could be better managed by other agencies or devolved to the private sector.

Conservatives also advocate for reforms that emphasize the importance of private property rights in agricultural policy. Farmers should have the freedom to make decisions about how to use their land, without being subjected to arbitrary or excessive government restrictions. Programs that restrict land use, such as conservation easements or wetlands regulations, should be carefully scrutinized to ensure they are not infringing on farmers' rights or limiting their ability to farm productively.

Conclusion

The conservative vision for the USDA emphasizes the need for reforming subsidy programs to reduce market distortions, removing unnecessary government intervention in farming practices, and limiting the influence of environmental activism on agricultural policy. By prioritizing the needs of farmers and fostering a more market-driven agricultural economy, the USDA can better support American agriculture's role as a global leader in food production. Reducing the regulatory burden and ensuring that the USDA respects the autonomy of American farmers will help to create a more efficient, resilient, and prosperous agricultural sector.

CHAPTER 7: EDUCATION AND WORKFORCE DEVELOPMENT

7.1 DEPARTMENT OF EDUCATION

Reducing Federal Influence in Education Policy

Conservatives have long argued for reducing the federal government's role in education, advocating for increased state and local control. The belief is that education is best managed by those closest to the students—local school districts, teachers, and parents—who are more aware of the needs and circumstances of their communities. This decentralization is intended to empower local entities to innovate and tailor education policies to serve their unique populations rather than adhering to broad federal mandates.

Historically, federal involvement in education has expanded, particularly with the passage of landmark legislation such as the Elementary and Secondary Education Act (ESEA) and No Child Left Behind (NCLB). These laws increased federal oversight by requiring states to meet national standards and benchmarks, often accompanied by federal funding contingent on compliance. However, this centralization is seen by conservatives as overreach, leading to a one-size-fits-all approach that stifles innovation and local control.

The conservative agenda aims to reduce this federal influence by rolling back national education programs and reducing the scope of the Department of Education. One key reform is shifting control of education funds to states through block grants, allowing states the flexibility to allocate resources in ways that best fit their needs. For example, the Academic Partnerships Lead Us to Success (APLUS) Act offers a model for this decentralization by giving states the option to opt out of federal education programs, while still receiving funding to apply to state-specific educational priorities.

School Choice and Education Savings Accounts

School choice is central to the conservative vision for education reform. It emphasizes empowering parents to choose the best educational environments for their children, whether that be public, charter, private, or homeschooling. Conservatives argue that competition among schools can drive innovation and improve educational outcomes, allowing families to escape failing school districts.

Education Savings Accounts (ESAs) are a tool to facilitate school choice. ESAs allow parents to direct public education funding toward alternative educational expenses such as private school tuition, tutoring, or online courses. Such programs have been successfully implemented in states like Arizona and Florida, where families can take control of their child's education and seek alternatives to traditional public schools. Federal support for these programs could include the creation of scholarship tax credits, encouraging donations to nonprofits that provide scholarships for low-income students to attend private schools.

Ending Federal Overreach in Education

Conservative education reform also seeks to end federal overreach, especially where it imposes policies that conflict with local values or priorities. For instance, under the Biden administration, federal funding for schools was tied to the adoption of policies related to equity, racial and gender inclusivity, and climate change education. Conservatives argue that these policies often push ideological agendas that are not aligned with the views of local communities.

Reforms include scaling back federal intervention in curriculum standards and data collection. Conservatives propose limiting the role of the Department of Education to areas such as data reporting and research dissemination, removing its influence over curriculum decisions and school operations. The goal is to eventually dismantle the Department of Education, shifting its responsibilities to the states and localities, while retaining a minimal federal role focused on protecting civil rights and ensuring transparency in educational outcomes.

7.2 DEPARTMENT OF LABOR

Promoting Pro-Family, Pro-Worker Policies

The Department of Labor under conservative leadership is focused on promoting policies that support American families and workers, while ensuring a business-friendly environment that fosters job creation. Conservatives advocate for policies that help workers balance family life with career opportunities, particularly by promoting flexible work arrangements and supporting labor market policies that encourage economic growth.

A key part of this vision is rejecting federal mandates that impose inflexible regulations on businesses, which conservatives argue can stifle economic opportunities and innovation. Instead, pro-family policies would include initiatives such as expanding access to paid family leave through voluntary, market-based solutions rather than government mandates.

Supporting Independent Workers and the Gig Economy

The rise of the gig economy has transformed the labor market, offering more Americans the ability to work as independent contractors or freelance workers. However, recent efforts to classify gig workers as traditional employees threaten to undermine the flexibility and autonomy that many workers value. Under the Biden administration, the Department of Labor moved to implement stricter guidelines that would force companies like Uber and Lyft to classify their drivers as employees, making them subject to labor laws around minimum wage, benefits, and collective bargaining.

Conservatives oppose these changes, advocating instead for protecting the rights of independent contractors. Policies like the Trump administration's proposed rule on the independent contractor test would ensure that workers can remain independent while enjoying the flexibility of contract work. The conservative stance is that labor laws should recognize and accommodate the diverse nature of modern work, offering protections without sacrificing the freedom that gig workers seek.

Reforming Union Influence and Labor Contracts

Unions have historically played a major role in American labor, but conservatives argue that current labor laws favor unions to the detriment of workers and businesses. For example, unionized workplaces often rely on closed shop agreements that force workers to join unions or pay union dues, even if they do not support the union's political or policy agendas. Right-to-work laws, which conservatives support, aim to eliminate this requirement, allowing workers to choose whether or not to join a union.

Additionally, conservatives believe that current labor laws make it difficult for workers to decertify unions or negotiate alternative forms of workplace representation. For instance, the contract bar rule prevents workers from removing a union during the life of a collective bargaining agreement. Reforms would aim to increase worker freedom by making it easier to vote out unions or adopt employee involvement organizations (EIOs), which allow for greater collaboration between workers and management without the adversarial nature of traditional unions.

Reducing Regulatory Burdens on Businesses

Conservative labor policy emphasizes reducing regulatory burdens that stifle business flexibility and competitiveness. Regulatory agencies like the Occupational Safety and Health Administration (OSHA) and the Equal Employment Opportunity Commission (EEOC) impose regulations that, while intended to protect workers, can often be overly broad or difficult for small businesses to comply with. Streamlining these regulations would allow businesses to operate more freely, particularly in areas like wage and hour laws, workplace safety, and discrimination policies.

For example, conservative reforms would include scaling back OSHA's expanded jurisdiction, allowing businesses greater freedom in managing workplace safety in ways that are tailored to their industries, rather than following prescriptive federal guidelines. Similarly, reducing the administrative burdens related to wage reporting, recordkeeping, and employee classification would make it easier for businesses to focus on growth and job creation.

Addressing Labor Negotiations and Union Contracts

Union contracts and collective bargaining agreements often place restrictions on businesses that can limit flexibility in managing their workforce. For instance, provisions like the prevailing wage requirements of the Davis-Bacon Act, which mandate that contractors on federal projects pay workers at union-level wages, increase costs for taxpayers and businesses. Conservatives argue that eliminating or reforming such requirements would allow for more competitive bidding on government contracts and reduce project costs.

Furthermore, addressing the issue of multiemployer pension plans, which are common in unionized industries, is another focus. Many of these plans are underfunded, creating long-term liabilities that could burden both businesses and taxpayers if federal bailouts are needed. Reforms would ensure that these plans are more financially sustainable, preventing future taxpayer bailouts.

Conclusion

In both education and labor policy, conservatives advocate for reducing federal overreach and promoting more localized control. In education, this means decentralizing the Department of Education's powers and giving states and parents more authority over school choice and curriculum decisions. In labor, the focus is on protecting worker freedoms, promoting flexibility in the workplace, and reducing burdensome regulations on businesses. Together, these reforms aim to create a more dynamic, competitive economy and a more effective education system that meets the diverse needs of American families and workers.

CHAPTER 8: PUBLIC HEALTH AND WELFARE

8.1 DEPARTMENT OF HEALTH AND HUMAN SERVICES (HHS)

Reforming Healthcare Policies to Reduce Dependency on Government Aid

The conservative approach to healthcare reform focuses on reducing the dependency on government assistance programs like Medicaid and the Affordable Care Act (ACA). These programs, while providing access to healthcare for millions, are seen by conservatives as fostering an over-reliance on government aid, contributing to long-term fiscal unsustainability, and inhibiting the growth of private healthcare markets.

To address this, the first step in reform involves restructuring federal healthcare programs to limit their scope and encourage personal responsibility. Conservatives argue for the introduction of block grants for Medicaid, transferring control over these funds to states. Under this model, states would have greater flexibility to design programs that meet the needs of their populations, without the stringent federal mandates that currently govern Medicaid. This decentralization would reduce the size of the federal bureaucracy and promote innovation at the state level.

In addition to Medicaid reform, conservatives advocate for scaling back certain aspects of the ACA, particularly the individual mandate, which required all Americans to purchase health insurance or face a tax penalty. By removing this requirement, individuals would have more freedom to choose whether or not to purchase insurance, relying on the market to offer a wider range of affordable healthcare plans. The goal is to shift from a government-driven system to one where the private market plays a more significant role in providing healthcare options.

Promoting Private Healthcare Solutions Over Government Programs

Conservatives prioritize private healthcare solutions as the foundation of a sustainable healthcare system. The belief is that private competition fosters innovation, improves quality, and reduces costs, whereas government-run systems create inefficiencies and limit consumer choice. This vision for healthcare reform focuses on empowering individuals to make healthcare decisions through Health Savings Accounts (HSAs) and high-deductible insurance plans, which incentivize personal responsibility and market competition.

HSAs allow individuals to save pre-tax dollars for medical expenses, making healthcare costs more manageable while reducing the reliance on insurance or government aid. Conservatives propose expanding the contribution limits for HSAs and increasing the number of eligible expenses, allowing individuals to use their accounts more flexibly. Additionally, pairing HSAs with high-deductible insurance plans offers consumers a lower-cost option for insurance, while encouraging them to be more conscious of healthcare spending decisions.

Another aspect of promoting private healthcare solutions is enhancing price transparency. Conservatives advocate for requiring hospitals and healthcare providers to publicly disclose the prices for common procedures and treatments, allowing consumers to compare costs and make informed choices. This transparency would promote competition, forcing providers to offer more competitive pricing and potentially lowering the overall cost of healthcare.

Interstate Health Insurance Markets

Another key reform involves allowing individuals to purchase health insurance across state lines. Currently, healthcare is regulated at the state level, which limits competition and choice. By allowing insurers to operate across state lines, conservatives argue that this would increase competition in the insurance market, leading to more affordable and diverse insurance options for consumers. Interstate health insurance markets would also prevent monopolies by reducing the dominance of a few insurance providers within individual states.

8.2 FOOD AND DRUG ADMINISTRATION (FDA)

Streamlining FDA Regulations to Encourage Medical Innovation

The Food and Drug Administration (FDA) plays a critical role in ensuring that medical products, including drugs and devices, are safe and effective for public use. However, conservatives argue that the FDA's regulatory process has become overly burdensome and slow, stifling medical innovation and delaying the availability of life-saving treatments. Streamlining FDA regulations is seen as a necessary step to encourage faster development and approval of medical products, thereby promoting innovation in the healthcare industry.

The conservative agenda proposes reforms to the FDA's approval processes, particularly for new drugs and medical devices. One of the primary goals is to reduce the time and cost associated with bringing new therapies to market. Currently, drug development can take over a decade and cost billions of dollars, a process that discourages innovation and limits the availability of new treatments. Conservatives argue that the FDA should adopt a more flexible, risk-based approach to regulation, focusing on safety and efficacy while reducing unnecessary bureaucratic hurdles.

Expedited Drug Approval Pathways

One area of focus is expanding the use of expedited approval pathways, such as the FDA's Breakthrough Therapy Designation and Fast Track programs. These pathways allow for the accelerated approval of drugs that show promise in treating serious or life-threatening conditions. While these programs have been successful in some cases, conservatives believe that they can be expanded further to ensure that more innovative therapies reach patients quickly.

For example, the 21st Century Cures Act, signed into law in 2016, aimed to accelerate medical product development by streamlining clinical trial processes and encouraging the use of real-world evidence in drug approvals. Conservatives propose building on this framework, giving the FDA more flexibility in how it evaluates new treatments, particularly for rare diseases and conditions with unmet medical needs.

Additionally, conservatives suggest that the FDA should allow for greater conditional approvals of drugs and devices, where products can be brought to market more quickly while continuing to gather data on their long-term efficacy. This approach balances the need for patient safety with the urgency of delivering innovative treatments to those who need them.

Fostering Competition in the Pharmaceutical Market

Another key reform involves encouraging competition in the pharmaceutical market by streamlining the approval process for generic drugs and biosimilars. Generic drugs, which are chemically identical to brand-name drugs but sold at a lower cost, play a crucial role in making medications more affordable. However, the FDA's approval process for generics can be slow and complex, leading to delays in the availability of these lower-cost alternatives.

By reforming the Hatch-Waxman Act—the law that governs generic drug approval—conservatives believe that the FDA can foster greater competition in the pharmaceutical market. This includes reducing the barriers to entry for generic manufacturers and addressing the use of patent gaming by brand-name drug companies, which extend their patents through minor modifications to delay generic competition.

Similarly, the FDA can encourage the use of biosimilars, which are near-identical versions of biologic drugs. Biologics, which are derived from living organisms, are some of the most expensive drugs on the market.

Expanding the availability of biosimilars would create more competition and reduce drug costs for patients.

Modernizing Clinical Trials

Clinical trials are a critical part of the drug development process, but conservatives argue that the current system is outdated and unnecessarily complex. One proposal for reform is to modernize clinical trials by incorporating adaptive trial designs and the use of real-world data. Adaptive trials allow for changes to the study design based on interim results, which can reduce the time and cost of trials while still maintaining scientific rigor.

The use of real-world evidence, which includes data collected from sources like electronic health records and insurance claims, can supplement traditional clinical trial data and provide a more comprehensive view of how drugs perform in everyday clinical settings. By integrating real-world evidence into the FDA's decision-making process, new treatments can be approved more quickly, without compromising safety.

Conclusion

Chapter 8 outlines a conservative approach to reforming healthcare and regulatory policies within the Department of Health and Human Services (HHS) and the Food and Drug Administration (FDA). For HHS, the focus is on reducing dependency on government programs and promoting private healthcare solutions, such as Health Savings Accounts and increased market competition. For the FDA, streamlining the regulatory process is crucial for fostering medical innovation, encouraging competition in the pharmaceutical market, and ensuring that life-saving treatments are approved and made available to patients more quickly. These reforms aim to create a healthcare system that is more efficient, competitive, and responsive to the needs of patients while minimizing government intervention.

CHAPTER 9:
INFRASTRUCTURE AND
TRANSPORTATION

9.1 DEPARTMENT OF
TRANSPORTATION (DOT)

Reversing Policies That Limit Freedom of Movement and Fuel Economy

The conservative approach to transportation policy centers on reducing government regulations that restrict personal freedom, particularly in relation to mobility and fuel economy standards. Under previous administrations, the Department of Transportation (DOT) implemented policies aimed at reducing carbon emissions, improving fuel efficiency, and transitioning the nation's transportation infrastructure toward a more environmentally sustainable model. These policies, while well-intentioned from an environmental perspective, are viewed by conservatives as overreaching, restrictive, and harmful to economic growth and individual freedom.

One such example is the increased Corporate Average Fuel Economy (CAFE) standards, which mandate that vehicles meet stringent fuel efficiency requirements. While these standards aim to reduce emissions and reliance on fossil fuels, they also increase the cost of producing vehicles, which is passed on to consumers. Furthermore, they limit the availability of certain vehicle types, particularly larger trucks and SUVs that many Americans prefer for their utility and comfort. Conservatives argue that these policies distort the vehicle market, force manufacturers to produce vehicles that may not meet consumer demand, and ultimately undermine the freedom of individuals to choose the types of vehicles they want to drive.

To reverse these trends, the conservative agenda proposes rolling back these fuel economy mandates and allowing the free market to determine vehicle production standards based on consumer preferences. This would not only lower the cost of vehicles but also ensure that Americans have greater freedom in selecting vehicles that suit their personal and professional needs. Conservatives argue that advancements in technology and market competition will naturally lead to improvements in fuel efficiency and vehicle performance without the need for government mandates.

Promoting Infrastructure That Facilitates Economic Growth and Personal Freedom

Conservatives emphasize that transportation infrastructure should facilitate economic growth by providing Americans with the freedom to move, trade, and work. Infrastructure is a crucial component of a thriving economy, and the DOT's primary responsibility should be to ensure that roads, highways, railways, and other transportation systems are well-maintained and efficient, without imposing unnecessary costs or restrictions on businesses and individuals.

Conservative reforms in infrastructure policy focus on reducing government overreach and bureaucracy in transportation projects. This includes reforming the

National Environmental Policy Act (NEPA) review process, which has become a significant barrier to the timely approval and completion of infrastructure projects. NEPA requires lengthy environmental impact assessments for new projects, which can delay construction for years and increase costs. Conservatives advocate for streamlining this process, reducing red tape, and setting firm deadlines for project approvals, ensuring that critical infrastructure projects are not unduly delayed.

In addition to reducing bureaucratic delays, conservatives believe in prioritizing infrastructure projects that provide a high return on investment and serve the broader needs of the economy. This means focusing on repairing and upgrading existing infrastructure, such as highways, bridges, and airports, rather than investing in politically driven projects like high-speed rail or public transit systems that have limited utility or economic value in certain regions.

Private sector involvement is also encouraged in the conservative vision for infrastructure development. Public-private partnerships (PPPs) are viewed as a way to leverage private capital and expertise to complete infrastructure projects more efficiently and cost-effectively than the government could manage on its own. By allowing private companies to invest in and manage transportation infrastructure, the government can reduce its financial burden while ensuring that infrastructure development is driven by market demand.

9.2 FEDERAL AVIATION ADMINISTRATION (FAA)

Reducing Regulatory Overhead in Aviation to Promote Industry Growth

The Federal Aviation Administration (FAA) is responsible for regulating and overseeing the aviation industry in the U.S., ensuring the safety and efficiency of air travel. However, conservatives argue that the FAA's regulatory approach has become overly burdensome, stifling innovation and growth in the aviation sector. To foster a more dynamic and competitive aviation industry, conservatives propose reforms that reduce regulatory overhead and promote a more flexible, market-driven approach to aviation management.

One of the primary areas of reform is air traffic control (ATC). Currently, the FAA manages the nation's ATC system, which is seen as outdated and inefficient compared to systems used in other countries. The conservative agenda supports privatizing air traffic control, shifting management responsibilities to a non-governmental organization or private entity. This would allow for faster adoption of modern technologies, such as satellite-based navigation systems, and improve the overall efficiency and safety of air travel. By reducing bureaucratic delays and inefficiencies, a privatized ATC system would enhance the competitiveness of the U.S. aviation industry and lower costs for airlines and passengers.

Regulatory Reform and Innovation in Aviation

The FAA's regulatory framework is often criticized for being slow to adapt to new technologies and business models in aviation. For example, the rise of drones and urban air mobility (UAM) vehicles presents new opportunities for growth in the aviation sector, but the FAA's current regulatory structure has struggled to keep pace with these innovations. Conservatives argue that the FAA should take a more flexible approach to regulation, allowing new technologies to be tested and deployed more quickly while maintaining safety standards.

To promote innovation, the FAA should create regulatory sandboxes, where companies can experiment with new aviation technologies in a controlled environment, without being subject to the full weight of federal regulations. These sandboxes would allow for the testing of commercial drone delivery systems, autonomous air taxis, and other emerging technologies, providing valuable data to inform future regulatory decisions.

Improving Competitiveness and Reducing Costs

Another area of focus is reducing the costs associated with aviation regulation. The FAA imposes a range of fees and compliance costs on airlines and other aviation businesses, which can limit industry growth and increase the cost of air travel for consumers. Conservatives advocate for reducing or eliminating unnecessary fees, streamlining the certification process for new aircraft and aviation technologies, and promoting competition in the industry.

Additionally, conservatives support efforts to encourage more competition among airports by promoting airport privatization. Many U.S. airports are publicly owned and operated, which can lead to inefficiencies and higher costs.

Privatizing airports, or allowing for greater private sector involvement in airport management, would introduce market pressures that could improve service quality, reduce operating costs, and increase investment in airport infrastructure.

Conclusion

Chapter 9 of the conservative agenda focuses on reforming infrastructure and transportation policies to promote economic growth, personal freedom, and industry innovation. For the Department of Transportation, this means reversing policies that limit freedom of movement and fuel economy choices, streamlining infrastructure development processes, and encouraging private sector involvement. For the FAA, reducing regulatory overhead, privatizing air traffic control, and promoting innovation in aviation are key strategies to foster a more competitive and dynamic aviation industry.

CHAPTER 10: LAW AND ORDER

10.1 DEPARTMENT OF JUSTICE (DOJ)

Ensuring Impartial Enforcement of Laws

A key focus of conservative reforms for the Department of Justice (DOJ) is ensuring that it enforces laws impartially, free from political bias. Over recent years, there has been increasing concern that the DOJ has become overly politicized, with accusations that it selectively enforces laws based on political considerations rather than legal principles. Conservatives argue that the DOJ should act as a neutral enforcer of the law, applying the law equally to all individuals and institutions, regardless of political affiliation.

To achieve this goal, reforms seek to restore the DOJ's credibility by implementing measures that insulate the department from political pressures. This includes stricter oversight of how investigations are initiated, particularly in politically sensitive cases, to ensure that decisions are based on evidence rather than partisan interests. Additionally, ensuring transparency in prosecutorial decisions is critical for restoring public trust. Conservatives propose reforms that would require the DOJ to provide clear justifications for its actions in high-profile cases, reducing the perception of favoritism or bias.

Another important aspect of these reforms is strengthening the Office of the Inspector General (OIG), which serves as an independent watchdog within the DOJ. By providing the OIG with greater autonomy and resources, the DOJ can ensure more robust internal oversight, preventing potential abuses of power and holding officials accountable for misconduct.

Reforming the DOJ's Approach to Civil Rights and Criminal Justice

Conservative reforms in the DOJ's approach to civil rights and criminal justice focus on ensuring fairness while respecting the rule of law. The goal is to move away from policies that emphasize group-based outcomes, and instead focus on individual rights and equal treatment under the law. Conservatives argue that the DOJ's civil rights division, in particular, has often overstepped its role by advancing politically charged policies on issues like race and gender, sometimes at the expense of other civil rights.

A key part of the reform agenda involves reorienting the DOJ's civil rights enforcement to focus on cases where there is clear evidence of individual discrimination, rather than pursuing broad policies that prioritize specific racial or demographic groups. This shift emphasizes protecting the rights of all individuals, regardless of their background, and ensuring that laws are applied fairly and impartially.

In criminal justice reform, conservatives support policies that balance public safety with fairness in sentencing and enforcement. This includes reforms to reduce disparities in sentencing for non-violent crimes, particularly drug-related offenses, which have disproportionately affected minority communities. At the same time, conservatives stress the importance of maintaining strong penalties for violent crime and repeat offenders, as public safety remains a priority.

There is also a focus on ensuring that the criminal justice system works efficiently and fairly for both victims and defendants. This includes efforts to reduce the backlog of cases in federal courts and improve the efficiency of the legal process through better use of technology and case management systems.

10.2 FEDERAL BUREAU OF INVESTIGATION (FBI)

Reforming Intelligence Operations to Focus on National Security Threats

The FBI plays a critical role in protecting the United States from national security threats, including terrorism, espionage, and cyberattacks. However, conservatives argue that in recent years, the FBI's focus has shifted away from these core responsibilities toward more politically sensitive domestic issues. This shift, they contend, has led to a misuse of the FBI's intelligence capabilities, which should be primarily directed at countering threats to national security.

One of the key reform proposals is to refocus the FBI's intelligence operations on identifying and neutralizing foreign and domestic threats to national security, such as terrorist organizations, foreign espionage, and cyberattacks by hostile actors. By redirecting resources toward these critical areas, the FBI can strengthen its ability to protect the nation from evolving security threats.

Reducing the FBI's Involvement in Domestic Political Issues

Conservatives have expressed concern about the FBI's involvement in politically charged investigations, particularly those related to domestic political figures and organizations. They argue that the FBI's involvement in these matters can lead to perceptions of bias and damage the bureau's credibility as an impartial law enforcement agency. To address this, conservatives propose reforms that would limit the FBI's role in investigating political figures unless there is clear evidence of criminal wrongdoing.

This includes stricter guidelines for initiating investigations that involve political campaigns, elected officials, or political organizations. By implementing higher standards of evidence for launching such investigations, the FBI can ensure that its resources are focused on genuine threats to national security and criminal activity, rather than being drawn into partisan conflicts.

Additionally, reforms propose increasing transparency in the FBI's activities, particularly when it comes to politically sensitive investigations. This could involve greater oversight by the DOJ's Office of the Inspector General (OIG) and more frequent reporting to Congress on the bureau's activities, ensuring that it remains accountable to both the public and the legislative branch.

Fostering Greater Accountability and Oversight

To improve the accountability of the FBI, conservatives propose enhancing external oversight mechanisms. This includes strengthening the role of the DOJ's Office of Professional Responsibility (OPR) and the Office of the Inspector General, which can investigate allegations of misconduct within the FBI. By ensuring that these offices have the authority and resources to conduct thorough investigations, the FBI can be held accountable for any abuses of power or lapses in its operations.

There is also support for reforming the Foreign Intelligence Surveillance Act (FISA) process, which governs the FBI's ability to conduct surveillance on individuals suspected of being involved in espionage or terrorism. Concerns have been raised about the potential for abuse of FISA warrants in politically sensitive cases, and conservatives argue that the process needs more rigorous oversight to prevent misuse. Proposals include requiring additional layers of judicial review and greater transparency in the FISA application process.

Conclusion

Chapter 10 highlights the need for reforms in both the Department of Justice and the FBI to ensure that they operate impartially and focus on their core responsibilities. For the DOJ, this means enforcing laws fairly without political bias and ensuring that civil rights and criminal justice policies are grounded in fairness and the rule of law. For the FBI, reforms aim to refocus intelligence operations on national security threats while reducing involvement in politically charged domestic issues. Both institutions would benefit from increased oversight and accountability, ensuring that they maintain the trust of the public and uphold their missions.

11.1 DEPARTMENT OF HOUSING AND URBAN DEVELOPMENT (HUD)

Refocusing HUD on its Core Mission of Housing for Citizens

The Department of Housing and Urban Development (HUD) was established to ensure that American citizens have access to safe, affordable housing. Over time, however, conservatives argue that HUD has experienced "mission creep," expanding its focus beyond its core mission into broader social policy areas that detract from its primary responsibilities. This mission creep has led to a growing bureaucracy and inefficiencies that undermine the department's effectiveness in addressing housing needs.

Conservative reforms seek to refocus HUD on its original mission: providing housing assistance to American citizens in need. This involves streamlining HUD's programs to ensure they are targeted at improving housing access and reducing homelessness, rather than being used as a vehicle for advancing broader social agendas. The goal is to reduce administrative overhead and eliminate programs that go beyond HUD's mandate, allowing the department to direct its resources toward those most in need of housing support.

The conservative vision emphasizes the importance of promoting self-reliance and individual responsibility in housing policies. This means prioritizing policies that encourage homeownership and financial independence, rather than long-term dependency on government housing assistance. Programs that promote affordable homeownership opportunities, such as public-private partnerships and housing vouchers, are central to this strategy. By working with private sector partners and local governments, HUD can help provide more housing options without expanding the federal government's role in housing development.

Preventing Mission Creep into Social Policies

Conservatives argue that HUD has increasingly become involved in areas of social policy that are outside its expertise, such as issues related to race, gender, and climate change. While these issues are important, they believe that HUD's involvement in such matters dilutes its focus and stretches its resources too thin. For example, recent initiatives aimed at promoting racial equity in housing or addressing climate change through housing regulations have been criticized as overreach that distracts from the department's primary goal of providing affordable housing to American citizens.

To address this, conservative reforms propose eliminating or significantly scaling back HUD's involvement in social policy areas that are better handled by other agencies or by state and local governments. This would allow HUD to concentrate its efforts on improving housing conditions and ensuring that resources are directed where they are most needed.

Ensuring that Federal Housing Assistance Goes to American Citizens

Another key aspect of conservative housing policy is ensuring that federal housing assistance is directed exclusively to American citizens. There is concern among conservatives that current policies allow noncitizens to access federal housing programs, which they argue diverts resources away from citizens who are most in need of assistance. By tightening eligibility requirements and improving oversight of housing programs, conservatives aim to ensure that federal housing assistance is reserved for American citizens.

This approach also involves enhancing verification processes to ensure that applicants for federal housing programs meet the necessary eligibility criteria. By implementing stricter guidelines and improving enforcement, HUD can better allocate its resources to American citizens who need housing assistance, while reducing the potential for fraud or misuse of federal funds.

Promoting Local Control and Innovation

In addition to refocusing HUD on its core mission, conservatives advocate for greater local control over housing programs. They argue that states and local governments are better equipped to understand the unique housing challenges in their communities and can implement policies that are more responsive to local needs. This could involve decentralizing certain HUD functions and giving local governments more flexibility in how they use federal housing funds, allowing for more innovation in addressing housing shortages and homelessness.

By fostering collaboration between the federal government, states, and localities, HUD can better support innovative solutions to housing challenges, such as affordable housing development, revitalization of distressed neighborhoods, and the reduction of homelessness.

Conclusion

The conservative vision for HUD is focused on returning the department to its core mission of providing housing assistance to American citizens while reducing its involvement in broader social policy initiatives. By streamlining programs, ensuring that federal resources are directed to citizens, and promoting local control, HUD can become more efficient and effective in addressing the nation's housing needs.

CHAPTER 12: FOREIGN POLICY AND INTERNATIONAL AID

12.1 DEPARTMENT OF STATE

Reaffirming the Importance of National Sovereignty in Foreign Policy

Conservative foreign policy emphasizes the primacy of national sovereignty, where the United States prioritizes its own interests and self-determination over the agendas of international organizations. In recent years, conservatives have grown increasingly concerned about the influence of global institutions, such as the United Nations (UN), the World Health Organization (WHO), and the International Monetary Fund (IMF), which they argue often promote policies that conflict with U.S. values or strategic goals.

To reaffirm national sovereignty, conservative policy proposals focus on limiting U.S. involvement in international organizations that are seen as overstepping their mandates or exerting undue influence over U.S. policy. While the U.S. will continue to honor its commitments to allies and engage in global diplomacy, conservatives seek to scale back participation in international agreements or treaties that constrain U.S. autonomy in areas such as defense, immigration, and trade.

A key component of this strategy is prioritizing bilateral relationships over multilateral arrangements. By focusing on direct, country-to-country negotiations, the U.S. can tailor its foreign policy to better serve its national interests, rather than being bound by broad, multilateral agreements that may not fully align with U.S. priorities. This shift would allow for more flexible, efficient diplomacy, enabling the U.S. to build stronger, mutually beneficial partnerships with allies while minimizing involvement in complex global bureaucracies.

Reducing the Emphasis on International Organizations

Conservatives argue that international organizations often fail to act in the best interests of the United States, particularly when their agendas are driven by non-elected bureaucrats or influenced by hostile or authoritarian regimes. In some cases, U.S. contributions to these organizations fund activities that undermine American values or strategic interests, such as support for human rights violators or ineffective peacekeeping missions.

To address this, conservative proposals advocate reducing financial contributions to international organizations that do not provide a clear benefit to the United States. Instead, the U.S. would focus on working with trusted allies through bilateral agreements or smaller coalitions of like-minded nations to achieve its foreign policy goals. By scaling back funding and participation in global institutions, the U.S. can assert its sovereignty and reduce its entanglements in foreign agendas.

Conservatives also call for reforming U.S. participation in organizations like the UN by promoting greater accountability and transparency in their operations. This includes pushing for reforms to the UN's decision-making processes to ensure that American values, such as democracy and individual rights, are upheld in the organization's policies.

12.2 UNITED STATES AGENCY FOR INTERNATIONAL DEVELOPMENT (USAID)

Aligning USAID's Efforts with American Interests

The United States Agency for International Development (USAID) has long been a key instrument of American foreign aid and development assistance. However, conservatives argue that USAID's mission has drifted over time, often prioritizing humanitarian and global development goals that do not always align with U.S. strategic interests. As a result, there is a push to realign USAID's efforts to better serve American geopolitical and economic objectives.

Under conservative reforms, USAID would focus on providing assistance to countries and regions that are of direct strategic importance to the United States. This includes supporting allies in key regions such as the Indo-Pacific, where competition with China is a top priority, and aiding countries that play a vital role in countering terrorism or advancing U.S. security interests. In regions where foreign aid has historically had little impact on U.S. security or economic prosperity, aid programs would be scaled back or eliminated.

A central principle of these reforms is ensuring that U.S. taxpayer dollars are spent wisely, with a clear return on investment in terms of advancing American interests. This means that foreign aid programs should be tied to specific objectives, such as promoting democracy, enhancing security, or creating economic opportunities for U.S. businesses. Aid recipients would be expected to meet certain benchmarks or conditions, such as demonstrating progress in governance or adopting pro-market reforms, to continue receiving U.S. assistance.

Reducing Foreign Aid Programs That Do Not Serve U.S. Goals

Conservative reforms advocate for cutting foreign aid programs that do not directly serve U.S. national interests or have failed to produce tangible results. Critics of USAID argue that too much foreign aid is allocated to programs that are inefficient, poorly managed, or directed at countries that are neither allies nor strategically important to the United States. In many cases, this aid has been seen as wasteful, with little oversight or accountability to ensure that it is used effectively.

To address these concerns, the conservative vision for USAID involves a thorough review of all foreign aid programs to determine their effectiveness and alignment with U.S. interests. Programs that fail to meet these criteria would be eliminated or significantly scaled back. Additionally, USAID would focus more on empowering local communities and fostering self-sufficiency in aid-receiving countries, reducing long-term dependency on U.S. assistance.

By focusing foreign aid on strategic interests, conservatives believe that the U.S. can maximize its influence abroad while minimizing unnecessary expenditures. This approach would also allow the U.S. to strengthen partnerships with countries that share its values and interests, ensuring that foreign aid serves as a tool for advancing American geopolitical objectives rather than a costly, unfocused humanitarian effort.

Conclusion

Chapter 12 highlights the conservative approach to foreign policy and international aid, which emphasizes national sovereignty, reducing reliance on international organizations, and focusing on bilateral relationships. For the Department of State, this means prioritizing direct diplomacy with key allies and reducing entanglements in multilateral agreements that do not serve U.S. interests. For USAID, reforms focus on aligning foreign aid programs with American strategic goals, ensuring that taxpayer dollars are spent efficiently and effectively in support of U.S. objectives.

CHAPTER 13: PROMOTING FREE ENTERPRISE AND SMALL BUSINESS

13.1 SMALL BUSINESS ADMINISTRATION (SBA)

The Small Business Administration (SBA) plays a crucial role in promoting entrepreneurship, providing support for small businesses, and fostering innovation. However, conservative reformers believe that the agency has become bogged down by inefficiencies, mismanagement, and the expansion of programs that do not adequately serve the small business community. The goal of reforming the SBA is to refocus the agency on its core mission: helping small businesses thrive and contribute to the free market, while reducing fraud and ensuring taxpayer dollars are used responsibly.

Reforming the SBA to Focus on Effective Programs

Over the years, the SBA has expanded its reach and scope, creating a wide array of programs designed to assist small businesses with funding, mentorship, and technical support. However, some of these programs have been criticized for being ineffective or too bureaucratic, resulting in inefficiencies that do not truly benefit the businesses they are intended to serve.

Conservatives advocate for a thorough review of all SBA programs to determine which ones are delivering tangible benefits to small businesses and which ones are duplicative, wasteful, or not aligned with the agency's mission. Programs that have outlived their usefulness or do not produce measurable results should be reformed or eliminated. This approach would allow the SBA to streamline its operations, focus on the most impactful initiatives, and ensure that resources are allocated to areas where they can provide the most value to small businesses.

Supporting Entrepreneurship and Free Markets

Central to the conservative approach is the belief that the government should play a limited role in the market. Rather than becoming a permanent fixture in the lives of small businesses, the SBA's primary role should be to provide targeted support that empowers entrepreneurs to succeed on their own. This includes offering loans, grants, and technical assistance to help businesses get off the ground, but without creating long-term dependency on government programs.

To promote entrepreneurship, conservatives propose that the SBA focus on programs that encourage innovation, competition, and self-sufficiency. For example, the Small Business Innovation Research (SBIR) and Small Business Technology Transfer (STTR) programs, which provide funding for research and development in high-tech industries, are seen as valuable tools for fostering innovation and helping small businesses compete in emerging markets. These programs should be preserved and enhanced, as they align with the goal of supporting entrepreneurship and driving economic growth through technological advancement.

On the other hand, conservatives argue that programs that do not directly contribute to economic growth or that foster dependency on government aid should be scaled back. The SBA's loan programs, for instance, should be restructured to ensure that they are helping businesses become financially independent, rather than relying on continuous government support. This means focusing on providing initial capital to help businesses start and grow, while encouraging them to transition to private financing as they become more established.

Enhancing Access to Capital for Small Businesses

One of the SBA's primary functions is providing access to capital for small businesses through its loan programs. These programs are critical for entrepreneurs who may not have access to traditional bank loans due to the risk associated with starting a new business. However, conservative reformers argue that the SBA's loan programs need to be reformed to ensure that they are serving their intended purpose without contributing to inefficiency or abuse.

The SBA's 7(a) Loan Program and 504 Loan Program are the two main vehicles for providing loans to small businesses. The 7(a) program is designed for general business purposes, while the 504 program is focused on real estate and equipment purchases. Both programs guarantee a portion of the loan made by private lenders, reducing the risk for banks and encouraging them to lend to small businesses.

While these programs are important for providing access to capital, there have been concerns about their effectiveness and the potential for mismanagement. Conservatives believe that reforms are needed to ensure that these programs are helping businesses that genuinely need assistance, rather than creating opportunities for fraud or misuse of funds.

Improving Oversight and Reducing Fraud

One of the most significant challenges facing the SBA is the issue of fraud and mismanagement within its loan programs. The Paycheck Protection Program (PPP), which was introduced during the COVID-19 pandemic to provide emergency loans to small businesses, exposed widespread fraud and abuse. Billions of dollars in loans were issued to fraudulent or ineligible businesses, leading to calls for better oversight and stricter controls.

To address these issues, conservatives propose reforms aimed at improving the SBA's ability to detect and prevent fraud in its loan programs. This includes enhancing the agency's verification processes for loan applicants, increasing the use of technology to identify potential red flags, and conducting more rigorous audits of businesses that receive SBA loans. By improving oversight and reducing opportunities for fraud, the SBA can ensure that its resources are directed toward legitimate small businesses that need assistance, rather than being wasted on fraudulent claims.

Another aspect of reducing fraud is ensuring that SBA loan programs are not being exploited by large companies or wealthy individuals. Critics argue that some SBA loans are being funneled to businesses that do not meet the traditional definition of a "small business," including companies with substantial assets or revenue. Conservatives advocate for stricter eligibility requirements to ensure that SBA loans are reserved for truly small businesses that would otherwise struggle to obtain financing.

Streamlining the SBA's Bureaucracy

Like many government agencies, the SBA has grown increasingly bureaucratic over time, with layers of administration that can slow down decision-making and reduce the efficiency of its programs. Conservatives argue that streamlining the SBA's bureaucracy is essential for making the agency more responsive to the needs of small businesses.

One proposal is to reduce the number of SBA programs that overlap with other federal or state initiatives. For example, many states have their own small business support programs, which often duplicate the services provided by the SBA. By consolidating or eliminating redundant programs, the SBA can focus its resources on areas where it is most needed and avoid unnecessary administrative costs.

Additionally, the SBA should improve its processes for handling loan applications and providing technical assistance. This could involve modernizing its IT systems, automating certain tasks, and reducing paperwork requirements for small businesses. By making the agency more efficient, the SBA can provide faster, more effective support to entrepreneurs and help them navigate the challenges of starting and growing a business.

Encouraging Private Sector Solutions

While the SBA plays an important role in supporting small businesses, conservatives believe that the private sector should take the lead in driving economic growth. Government programs, they argue, should complement—not replace—private sector initiatives. To this end, reforms to the SBA should focus on encouraging private sector investment in small businesses and reducing the agency's footprint over time.

One way to achieve this is through public-private partnerships (PPPs), which leverage private capital to fund small business development projects. PPPs can help reduce the reliance on government funding while fostering innovation and entrepreneurship in the private sector. Additionally, the SBA can work with private lenders to expand access to capital for small businesses, providing guarantees or incentives to encourage more private lending rather than relying solely on government-backed loans.

Conservatives also support reducing the SBA's role in direct lending and shifting more responsibility to private lenders. By encouraging private banks and financial institutions to take on more of the lending risk, the SBA can focus on its role as a facilitator rather than a primary source of capital. This approach would help reduce the federal government's financial exposure while promoting a more market-driven approach to small business financing.

Conclusion

Reforming the Small Business Administration is a key priority for conservatives who believe that the agency should be more focused, efficient, and aligned with the principles of free enterprise. By streamlining its programs, reducing fraud, and encouraging private sector solutions, the SBA can better serve the needs of small businesses while minimizing the burden on taxpayers. The goal is to create a more dynamic, competitive economy where entrepreneurs can thrive without becoming overly reliant on government assistance. Through these reforms, the SBA can play a vital role in promoting innovation, job creation, and economic growth, while ensuring that taxpayer dollars are used responsibly and effectively.

Made in the USA
Monee, IL
03 October 2024

67115357R00059